trEATs

trEATs

Delicious food gifts to make at home

APRIL CARTER

hardie grant books
MELBOURNE · LONDON

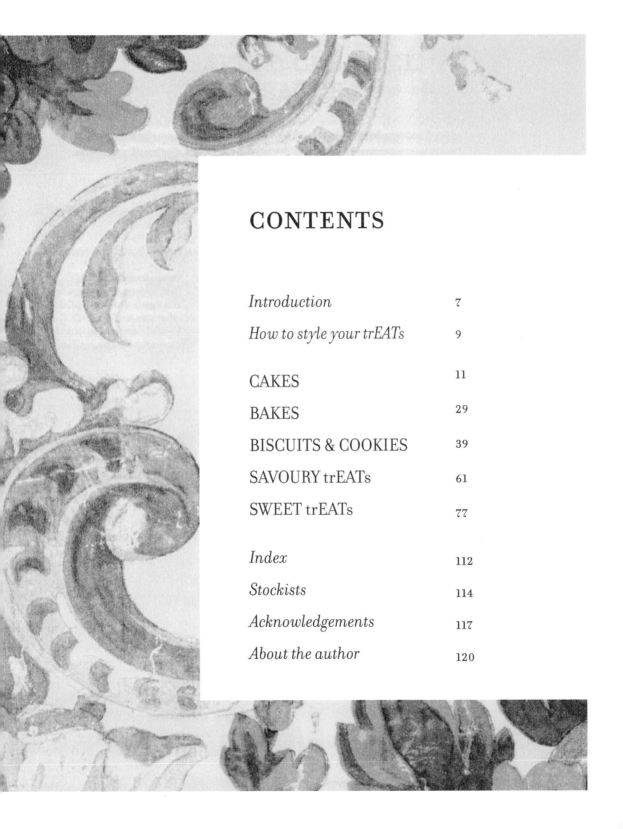

CONTENTS

INTRODUCTION

One of my favourite things about baking is getting to share what I've made. Whether it's a gift to say thank you, a way of celebrating happy news or something sweet to cheer up a friend, thoughtful, beautifully presented trEATs that taste as good as they look have a way of making people feel happy. Of course, you also get to sample lots of different recipes without the temptation of eating the whole batch yourself!

Most of us don't have time to spend hours in the kitchen, so with that in mind you'll find plenty of simple and quick recipes in this book that don't use too many different ingredients. The White Chocolate & Pistachio Popcorn recipe (page 99) can be put together just before you go out, Gingerbread Bats (page 45) can be baked in advance and decorated later, and the Pomegranate & Vanilla Vodka (page 109) can be made a couple of weeks ahead. Everyone appreciates the time that goes into making something lovely at home, even if it's just an hour squeezed in at the weekend or a late-night baking session after work.

Make your trEATs even more thoughtful by customising what you make — swap the dark chocolate in the Chocolate Chip Cookies (page 46) for white chocolate, up the chilli powder in the Smoked Paprika Almonds (page 68), or choose a favourite colour for the Dipped & Decorated Marshmallows (page 90).

After all of your effort in the kitchen, it's really fun to show off your trEATs with beautiful packaging and presentation. I always think that simple is best when it comes to food packaging and that you don't need anything too fussy or expensive. I keep a good supply of baker's twine in three different colours, some baking paper, medium-sized cellophane bags and some deli-style paper bags for keeping things flat. As well as the 'How to style your trEATs' information overleaf, you'll find lots of tips for packaging and styling your gifts with each recipe.

Most of all, have fun baking, making and sharing, and remember to keep a few trEATs for yourself as well.

HOW TO STYLE YOUR trEATS

Beautiful styling can make such a difference. By thinking about how to package up your trEATs you'll not only make sure that they get to their destination in one piece, but you can turn your batch of simple popcorn or cheese straws into a thoughtful and stylish gift.

When it comes to choosing packaging you don't need to buy anything too expensive. Try to keep some baking paper, baker's twine, cellophane bags and an empty jar or two to hand and you'll be covered for most of the recipes in this book.

Looking out for deli-style paper bags, cartons and cake boxes means that you won't be stuck carrying empty cake tins home at the end of an evening. A cake box tied with string like an old-fashioned parcel is one of the best ways of keeping cakes flat whether you're travelling by car or public transport. Patisserie bags with wide bases are useful for keeping boxes the right way up, and cotton tote bags can be folded away for the journey home.

If you're making something for a special present, try to find vintage tins, unusual boxes or even egg cartons to package your trEATs in. Line boxes and tins with baking, craft or tissue paper and separate individual cakes and biscuits with cupcake cases or squares of baking paper.

Personalise your trEATs by hand-writing a message on a parcel tag tied with ribbon or string, or take a tip from artisan bakeries and use a rubber stamping set to print the name of the trEAT or person it's intended for directly onto the paper, box or bag. Making labels for your cakes, biscuits and foodie gifts is a great excuse to buy nice stationery.

Pairing different gifts can be a really fun way to give food too. Think about packaging up the Oatcakes with Pink Peppercorns (page 67) with an artisan cheese, or the Currant Scones (page 36) with some jam. Look out for unusual boxes or tins and make up your own cookie selection – try arranging the Tiny Lemon Meringue Pie Cookies (page 48) on one side of the tin with the Blackberry and Vanilla Linzer Cookies (page 40) on the other. Or make sweet suggestions for how to eat each trEAT; one of the simplest and most personal foodie gifts that I've received was some dark wasabi-flavoured chocolate with a hand-written note on it that said 'to be enjoyed with your evening green tea' – one of my favourite drinks to have with chocolate.

CAKES

CHERRY & CINNAMON BUNDT CAKES

These delicious delights make an elegant accompaniment to a cup of tea. Add more fresh cherries when you're packaging them up as a gift to inject a good splash of ruby-red colour.

Makes 12

125 g (4 oz) unsalted butter, plus extra for greasing
125 g (4 oz/⅔ cup) light brown soft sugar
50 g (2 oz/⅖ cup) caster (superfine) sugar
2 large (US – extra large) eggs
175 g (6 oz/1⅖ cups) plain (all-purpose) flour
½ teaspoon baking powder
2 teaspoons ground cinnamon
pinch of salt
125 ml (4 fl oz) milk
½ teaspoon vanilla extract
200 g (7 oz) fresh cherries, pitted and quartered
icing (confectioner's) sugar for dusting

Preheat the oven to 170°C (340°F/gas mark 3) and lightly butter a 12-hole mini bundt tin.

Using a food processor with the beater attachment, beat the butter and sugars until the mixture is pale and creamy. Add the eggs one at a time, beating after each addition until they're well incorporated into the mixture.

Into a clean bowl sift the flour, baking powder, cinnamon and salt, and stir to combine. Add half the flour mixture to the butter mixture in the food processor and beat. Add the milk and vanilla extract, continuing to beat, and then add the remaining flour mixture and beat until just combined – do not over-beat. Finally, fold in the cherries.

Take your prepared 12-hole mini bundt tin and spoon the mixture into each bundt hole, until each hole is two-thirds full. Bake for 25 minutes, or until a skewer inserted into the centre of one of the cakes comes out clean.

Allow the cakes to fully cool in the tin, then turn them out onto a wire rack and dust with icing sugar. Store in a tin or an airtight container for up to 3 days.

BROWNIES WITH SALTED CARAMEL

These brownies are really easy to make and the oozy salted caramel gives them an extra drizzle of decadence. Layer them between squares of baking paper to stop them from sticking together, and take them to a friend's for dinner as an easy-to-transport dessert. Serve with ice cream and some warmed caramel on the side. To make the Salted Caramel Sauce, see page 89. Alternatively, use a shop-bought one.

MAKES 9 LARGE BROWNIES OR
16 SMALLER ONES

150 g (5 oz) unsalted butter, cubed
150 g (5 oz) dark chocolate,
  finely chopped
300 g (10½ oz/1³⁄₁₀ cups)
  caster (superfine) sugar
100 g (3½ oz/½ cup) dark
  brown soft sugar
3 large (US – extra large) eggs
1 teaspoon vanilla extract
150 g (5 oz/1⅕ cups) plain
  (all-purpose) flour
½ teaspoon salt
2 tablespoons Salted Caramel
  Sauce (page 89), warmed

Preheat the oven to 170°C (340°F/gas mark 3). Butter a 20 × 20 cm (8 × 8 in) square baking tin and line it with baking paper.

Melt the butter and chocolate in a glass bowl over a saucepan of simmering water, ensuring that the water doesn't touch the bottom of the bowl. Stir until the mixture is almost melted, then remove the pan from the heat. Remove the glass bowl from the saucepan to ensure that the chocolate doesn't become overheated, and continue to stir the mixture until the chocolate is completely melted. Put the bowl to one side and allow it to cool slightly.

Meanwhile, using the whisk attachment of a food processor, whisk the sugars, eggs and vanilla extract until the mixture is light and foamy. Continue to whisk as you add the melted chocolate mixture. In a separate clean bowl sift the flour and salt, then gradually fold it in to the chocolate mixture until the ingredients are just combined – do not over-mix.

Pour the mixture into the prepared tin. Drizzle the salted caramel sauce over the top. Bake in the oven for 30 minutes: the sides and top should be set and the centre still moist.

Allow to cool in the tin before cutting into squares. Store in an airtight container for up to a week.

ALMOND & EARL GREY TEACUP CAKES

These moist almond cakes are delicately flavoured with Earl Grey tea, which gives them a floral edge. Most teacups should be able to withstand oven temperatures but don't risk your best china. These teacup cakes make brilliant gifts, especially if the recipient gets to keep the teacup too.

MAKES 8

FOR THE CAKES
120 ml (4 fl oz) milk
½ teaspoon vanilla extract
3 Earl Grey tea bags
120 g (4 oz) unsalted butter
225 g (8 oz/1 cup) caster (superfine) sugar
2 large (US – extra large) eggs
100 g (3½ oz/⅘ cup) plain (all-purpose) flour
75 g (2½ oz) ground almonds
1 teaspoon baking powder

FOR THE TOPPING
50 g (2 oz) flaked almonds
125 g (4 oz/1 cup) icing (confectioner's) sugar, plus extra for dusting
4–5 teaspoons warm water

Preheat the oven to 170°C (340°F/gas mark 3). Butter 8 teacups or ramekins with 120 ml (4 fl oz) capacity, and place them on a baking tray.

Warm the milk, vanilla and tea bags in a small saucepan over a medium heat until the liquid is just bubbling. Set aside to cool.

Using a food processor with the beater attachment, beat the butter and sugar until the mixture is pale and creamy. Add the eggs to the butter mixture one at a time, beating after each addition until they are well incorporated.

Into a clean bowl sift the flour, ground almonds and baking powder, and stir to combine. Then, remove the tea bags from the cooled milk, making sure you squeeze them first to extract all of the flavour. Still using the food processor, beat in half of the flour mixture to the butter mixture, and then beat in half of the milk mixture. Repeat with the rest of each mixture and scrape down the sides of the mixing bowl to make sure that all of the ingredients are well incorporated.

Divide the mixture between the teacups or ramekins, filling each one until it is two-thirds full. Bake for 18–20 minutes, until the cakes are golden brown and springy to the touch.

Set them aside to cool.

Leave the oven on at 170°C (340°F/gas mark 3). While your teacup cakes are cooling, you can toast the almonds: place them on a baking tray and bake in the oven for 8–10 minutes, or until they're golden brown.

Next, it's time to make the glaze, which is as easy as combining the icing sugar with the warm water in a bowl.

Once your teacup cakes are completely cooled, you can decorate them with the topping: drizzle the glaze over the top of each cake, then finish with a sprinkle of toasted almonds and a dusting of icing sugar. Store in a tin or an airtight container for up to 3 days.

ROSE- & LEAF-TOPPED CAKE POPS

I made these for a friend's wedding, each cake pop individually wrapped in a little cellophane bag and tied with green and white baker's twine for guests to enjoy on their way home – the perfect trEAT. Cake pops take a while to put together but they always impress, so are well worth the effort. You will need a silicone mould to make the roses and a cutter to make the leaves, but if you can't source them, they are just as good without. They will keep in the fridge for up to a week.

MAKES 20

FOR THE RED VELVET CAKE
60 g (2 oz) unsalted butter,
  plus extra for greasing
150 g (5 oz/⅔ cup) caster
  (superfine) sugar
1 large (US – extra large) egg
1 tablespoon cocoa powder
150 g (5 oz/1⅕ cups) plain
  (all-purpose) flour
120 ml (4 fl oz) milk
1 tablespoon red food colouring
½ teaspoon vanilla extract
½ teaspoon salt
½ teaspoon bicarbonate of soda
1½ teaspoons white wine vinegar

FOR THE FROSTING
80 g (3 oz/⅔ cup) icing
  (confectioner's) sugar
40 g (1½ oz) cream cheese

FOR THE DECORATIONS
100 g (3½ oz) white sugar
  paste (fondant)
½ teaspoon CMC powder
a few drops of green food
  colouring
icing (confectioner's) sugar
  for dusting
gold lustre dust
2–3 drops rejuvenator spirit,
  or vodka

FOR THE CAKE POPS
400 g (14 oz) light green
  candy melts
1–3 tablespoons vegetable oil
20 x 15 cm (6 in) lollipop sticks

To make the cake, preheat the oven to 170°C (340°F/gas mark 3). Lightly butter a 20 cm (8 in) diameter round cake tin and line it with baking paper.

Using a food processor with the beater attachment, beat together the butter and sugar until the mixture is pale and creamy. Add the egg and beat until it is well incorporated. Sift the flour and cocoa together into a separate clean bowl. Measure out the milk and add the food colouring and vanilla extract. Add the flour and milk mixtures to the butter mixture, half at a time. Finally, add the salt, bicarbonate of soda and white wine vinegar and beat using the food processor until they are well incorporated. Scrape down the sides of the bowl to make sure that all of the ingredients are well mixed. Pour the mixture into the prepared tin and bake in the oven for 30 minutes, or until a skewer inserted in the centre comes out clean. Set the cake aside to fully cool in the tin. Once cooled, break the cake up into crumbs.

To make the cream-cheese frosting, use a food processor to beat the icing sugar and cream cheese together until smooth. Set it aside with your cake.

To make the rose and leaf decorations, knead the CMC powder into the sugar paste, then divide into two halves. Use the food colouring to colour one half green. Dust the work surface with icing sugar, then roll out the green sugar paste to 3–4 mm (⅕ in). Use a small leaf cutter to cut out leaf shapes. Divide up the remaining sugar paste into 2 cm (¾ in) balls and press into a small silicone rose mould to make the sugar roses. Set the roses and leaves aside for 15–20 minutes to firm up. Once firm, mix a little gold lustre dust in a small bowl with a few drops of rejuvenator spirit or vodka to form a paste. Use a paintbrush to paint your sugar roses gold.

To make your cake pops, first, line a baking tray with baking paper. Then, mix the cake crumbs in a large bowl with the frosting to form a dough. Roll the dough into 20 balls, approximately 30 g (1 oz) each in weight, and place them on the lined tray. Cover with clingfilm and chill for 2 hours, or until firm. Once firm, remove the cake balls from the fridge. Melt the candy melts by following the instructions on the packet and stir in the oil until the candy is smooth and runny. Set aside to cool slightly.

When the candy has cooled, dip the end of each lollipop stick 1 cm (½ in) into the candy, and insert the stick halfway into each cake ball. Then, carefully dip each cake ball in the candy until it reaches the stick, and gently tap off the excess. Place your cake pops in a polystyrene block to hold them upright, decorate with a rose or leaf, and set aside to dry.

SPICED PEAR & CHOCOLATE CAKES

The poached pears in these cakes are sweet and fragrant. You can give them as a gift in their own right in a big, syrup-filled preserving jar as well as baking them into these individual chocolate cakes. Present the cakes still in their ramekins, or turned out and wrapped in brown muffin wrappers.

MAKES 6

FOR THE SPICED PEARS
6 small, firm pears
500 g (1 lb 2 oz/2¼ cups) caster (superfine) sugar
1 litre cold water
10 cloves
10 cardamom pods
2 cinnamon sticks

FOR THE CHOCOLATE CAKES
25 g (1 oz) cocoa powder
1 teaspoon vanilla extract
4 tablespoons boiling water
60 g (2 oz) unsalted butter, plus extra for greasing
50 g (2 oz/¼ cup) caster (superfine) sugar
50 g (2 oz/¼ cup) dark brown soft sugar
1 large (US – extra large) egg
2 tablespoons milk
90 g (3¼ oz/¾ cup) plain (all-purpose) flour
1 teaspoon baking powder
¼ teaspoon salt
icing (confectioner's) sugar, for dusting

Peel the pears, leaving the stalks intact, then slice off the bottoms and hollow out to remove the core and seeds.

Place the sugar and water in a large saucepan and bring to the boil. Continue boiling until the sugar has dissolved. Then, add all of the spices and pears to the saucepan and reduce to a simmer. To keep the pears submerged, place some baking paper onto the surface of the syrup and weigh down with a small saucepan lid or plate that fits inside the saucepan. Simmer for 15 minutes, or until the pears are tender. Leave the pears in the syrup and set aside to cool.

Meanwhile, start making your chocolate cakes. Preheat the oven to 170°C (340°F/gas mark 3). Lightly butter 6 ramekins with 120 ml (4 fl oz) capacity, and place them on a baking tray. Mix the cocoa powder, vanilla extract and boiling water in a small bowl until the ingredients are combined, and then set aside to cool.

Using a food processor with the beater attachment, beat the butter and sugars together for 3–4 minutes, or until the mixture is pale and creamy. Add the egg and milk to the butter mixture and beat well.

Into a clean bowl sift the the flour, baking powder and salt, and stir to combine. Still using the food processor, beat in half of the flour mixture to the butter mixture, and then beat in half of the cooled cocoa mixture. Repeat with the rest of each mixture and scrape down the sides of the mixing bowl to make sure that all of the ingredients are well incorporated.

Divide the mixture between the ramekins and press one of the pears into the centre of each. The cake mixture should come about halfway up each pear. Bake for 18–20 minutes, or until a skewer inserted into one of the cakes comes out clean.

Cool the cakes on a wire rack and dust with icing sugar. Store in a tin or an airtight container for up to 3 days. Serve at room temperature.

RASPBERRY, ROSE & CHOCOLATE CUPCAKES

Pretty pastel colours are a popular way to decorate cupcakes, but I also love tinting buttercream this beautifully bold deep pink to complement the raspberry and rose flavours. You can buy special cupcake boxes that fit six, twelve or even single cupcakes to package these in – seek out brown or black boxes and cupcake cases for a modern look.

FOR THE CHOCOLATE CAKES
50 g (2 oz) cocoa powder
1½ teaspoons vanilla extract
125ml (4 fl oz) boiling water
110 g (3¾ oz) unsalted butter
100 g (3½ oz/⅖ cup)
   caster (superfine) sugar
100 g (3½ oz/½ cup) dark
   brown soft sugar
2 large (US – extra large) eggs
175 g (6 oz/1⅖ cup) plain
   (all-purpose) flour
2 teaspoons baking powder
½ teaspoon salt
60 ml (2 fl oz) milk

FOR THE RASPBERRY FILLING
4 tablespoons raspberry jam

FOR THE ROSE BUTTERCREAM
125 g (4 oz) unsalted butter
250 g (9 oz/2 cups) icing
   (confectioner's) sugar
2 teaspoons milk
3 drops of rose extract
claret or pink gel food colouring

To make the cakes, preheat the oven to 170°C (340°F/gas mark 3). Line a 12-hole cupcake tin with cupcake cases. Mix the cocoa powder, vanilla extract and boiling water in a small bowl until combined, then set aside to cool.

Using a food processor with the beater attachment, beat the butter and sugars in a bowl for 3–4 minutes, or until the mixture is pale and creamy. Add the eggs to the butter mixture, one at a time, and beat well after each addition.

Into a clean bowl sift the the flour, baking powder and salt and stir to combine. Add to the butter mixture, along with the milk and the cocoa mixture, and use the food processor to beat it all together. Scrape down the sides of the bowl to make sure that all of the ingredients are well incorporated, then divide the mixture between the cupcake cases until each one is two-thirds full. Bake for 18–20 minutes, or until a skewer inserted into one of the cakes comes out clean.

Remove the cakes from the cupcake tin and set aside to cool.

To make the buttercream, place all of the ingredients into a bowl and use a food processor to beat them together for 4–5 minutes, or until pale and creamy.

Once the cakes have cooled, cut a small, cone-shaped, 2 cm (¾ in) deep piece from the top of each cake. Fill each hole with a teaspoon of jam and top with the cut-out piece. Then, pipe the rose buttercream onto the top of each cake using a large star tip. To pipe a rose design, start piping from the centre of each cake and spiral outwards.

Cover and store in the fridge for up to 3 days. Any leftover buttercream can be stored in an airtight container in the fridge for up to 2 weeks.

CHOCOLATE EASTER-EGG CAKES

These are the perfect Easter trEAT, and egg cartons are a fun way to transport your mini-sized cakes in handy half-dozen or dozen batches. Recycle your leftover cartons, or look online for different coloured cartons to purchase. Pop the cakes into paper cases to make them easier to lift out and eat.

MAKES 24

FOR THE CHOCOLATE CAKE
50 g (2 oz) cocoa powder
1½ teaspoons vanilla extract
125 ml (4¼ fl oz) boiling water
175 g (6 oz/1⅖ cup) plain
  (all-purpose) flour
2 teaspoons baking powder
½ teaspoon salt
110 g (3¾ oz) unsalted butter
100 g (3½ oz/⅖ cup)
  caster (superfine) sugar
100 g (3½ oz/⅖ cup) dark
  brown soft sugar
2 large (US – extra large) eggs
60 ml (2 fl oz) milk

FOR THE GANACHE
75 g (2½ oz) dark chocolate,
  chopped into small pieces
75 ml (2½ fl oz) double
  (thick) cream

TO DECORATE
24 mini chocolate eggs

Preheat the oven to 170°C (340°F/gas mark 3).

Lightly butter and line a 20 x 20 cm (8 x 8 in) square cake tin. Mix the cocoa powder, vanilla extract and boiling water in a small bowl until combined, then set aside to cool. Into a clean bowl sift the flour, baking powder and salt, stir to combine and set aside.

Using a food processor with the beater attachment, beat the butter and sugars for 3–4 minutes, or until the mixture is pale and creamy. Add the eggs to the butter mixture, beating well after each addition. Add the milk, plus the cocoa and flour mixtures, and continue to beat. Scrape down the sides of the bowl to make sure that all of the ingredients are well incorporated.

Pour the mixture into the prepared tin and bake for 20–25 minutes, or until a skewer inserted into the cake comes out clean.

Remove from the tin and set the cake aside to cool on a wire rack.

To make the ganache, place the chopped chocolate in a bowl. Heat the cream in a saucepan until it is bubbling, and then pour the cream over the chocolate. Whisk until it is completely smooth and all of the chocolate has melted. Set aside to cool, then chill for 20 minutes, or until thickened. Once your chilled ganache has thickened, beat with a spatula until it is smooth.

To assemble the cakes, cut out small shapes using a round 3 cm (1 in) cutter. Use a spatula or knife to frost the cakes with the ganache. Place each cake in a mini cupcake case and decorate with a mini chocolate egg. Store in a tin or an airtight container in the fridge for up to 3 days. Serve at room temperature.

COCONUT
MADELEINES

These pretty French trEATs are best eaten on the day you bake them, but the cake mixture can be made the night before. I love the shell designs of traditional madeleine tins, but you can also bake these in a mini muffin tin. Package up these melt-in-the-mouth trEATs in a tin to keep them fresh, and hand-write a label with 'eat me' to encourage swift eating.

Makes 24

3 large (US – extra large) eggs
120 g (4 oz/½ cup) caster (superfine) sugar
150 g (5 oz) butter, melted and cooled, plus extra for greasing
5 tablespoons milk
150 g (5 oz/1⅕ cups) plain (all-purpose) flour
½ teaspoon baking powder
100 g (3½ oz) desiccated coconut
icing (confectioner's) sugar for dusting

Preheat the oven to 170°C (340°F/gas mark 3) and brush a 12-shell madeleine tin with some melted butter. Using a food processor with the whisk attachment, whisk the eggs and sugar together for 3–4 minutes, or until the mixture is frothy. Combine the melted butter with the milk and whisk into the egg mixture.

Into a clean bowl sift the flour and baking powder and combine with the coconut. Fold the flour mixture into the egg mixture. Scrape down the sides of the bowl to make sure that all of the ingredients are well incorporated. Cover the bowl and chill for 20 minutes – this ensures that the madeleines rise properly in the oven.

The mixture makes 24, so you will need to bake these in 2 batches. Using half the mixture, fill each madeleine shell until it is two-thirds full.

Bake for 8–10 minutes, or until the madeleines have risen and are springy to the touch. Remove the madeleines from the tin to cool, and repeat with the remaining mixture. Cool the madeleines on a wire rack and dust with icing sugar. Store in a tin or an airtight container for up to 3 days.

BAKES

GLAZED MINI RING DOUGHNUTS

These doughnuts have an iconic cartoon cuteness about them. To make them ring shaped, you need a special doughnut pan, but there's no proving or frying involved so they're really easy. Have fun dipping them in different colour glazes, and get out your sprinkles collection for colourful decoration. Alternatively, skip the glaze and dip them in sugar and cinnamon while they're still warm from the oven.

MAKES 48

150 ml (5 fl oz) milk
1 large (US – extra large) egg
30 g (1 oz) unsalted butter, melted and cooled slightly, plus extra for greasing
½ teaspoon vanilla extract
180 g (6 oz/1⅖ cups) plain (all-purpose) flour
75 g (2½ oz/⅓ cup) caster (superfine) sugar
1 teaspoon baking powder
pinch of ground nutmeg
½ teaspoon ground cinnamon
½ teaspoon salt

FOR THE GLAZE

200 g (7 oz/1⅗ cups) icing (confectioner's) sugar
2–3 tablespoons water
a few drops of pink food colouring
sprinkles to decorate

Preheat the oven to 180°C (350°F/gas mark 4) and lightly butter a 12-hole mini doughnut pan. Using a food processor, beat the milk, egg, butter and vanilla extract until they're well combined.

Into a clean bowl sift the flour, sugar, baking powder, nutmeg, cinnamon and salt, and stir to combine. Add the flour mixture to the butter mixture in the food processor and whisk until it is just incorporated – do not over-mix.

This recipe makes 48 mini doughnuts, so you will need to bake them in batches. Pour the mixture into the mini doughnut pan, ensuring each ring is about half full. Bake in the oven for 8 minutes, or until golden brown and springy to the touch.

Remove the doughnuts from the tin and allow them to cool on a wire rack. Repeat with the remaining mixture.

To make the glaze, whisk the icing sugar, water and a drop or two of food colouring in a bowl. Dip one side of each doughnut into the glaze and shake off the excess. Decorate with the sprinkles and leave to set on a wire rack, with some baking paper underneath to catch any drips. Though best eaten fresh, you can store the doughnuts in a tin or an airtight container for up to 3 days.

MINI MINCE PIES

I make a big batch of these every year and split them between tins to make sure I have enough for the different festive visits to family and friends. Try to find some snowflake-like paper doilies to line your tins with, and give the finished pies a dusting of icing sugar for that final snowy touch.

Makes 24

250 g (9 oz/2 cups) plain (all-purpose) flour
125 g (4 oz) unsalted butter, cubed and chilled
pinch of salt
3–4 tablespoons ice-cold water
1 x 410 g (14 oz) jar of mincemeat
1 large (US – extra large) egg, beaten
icing (confectioner's) sugar for dusting

To make the pastry, place the flour, butter and salt in the bowl of a food processor and mix for 20 seconds, or until the mixture looks like breadcrumbs. Add the cold water and mix again, just enough until it forms a ball. Turn the dough out of the bowl, wrap in clingfilm and chill in the fridge for 30 minutes.

Preheat the oven to 200°C (400°F/gas mark 6). Roll the chilled pastry out onto a floured surface until it is as thin as possible, and cut out 24 circles using a 7 cm (2¾ in) pastry cutter. Line a 24-hole mini-muffin tin with your pastry circles, and chill for 10 minutes.

Roll out the remaining pastry and use a 4.5 cm (2 in) circle- or star-shaped cutter for the lids.

Remove your pastry-lined mini-muffin tin from the fridge, and divide the mincemeat between the cases, filling each to three-quarters full. Brush the tops of the pastry cases with the beaten egg and press the pastry lids on top. Seal each pie by pressing the edges with a fork. Brush the tops of the pies with the egg and bake for 20 minutes, or until golden brown.

Cool the pies on a wire rack and dust with icing sugar.

PLUM CRUMBLE IN A JAR & APPLE PIE IN A JAR

Baking these tasty puddings in jars makes them really easy to transport – just pop the lid on and you can take them to friends' houses as an after-dinner trEAT, or share them cold at a picnic. Look out for shallow 'terrine'-style preserving jars, which are easier to get eager spoons into.

MAKES 4 OF EACH (8 IN ALL)

FOR THE PLUM CRUMBLE FILLING

16 plums, halved with stones removed
75 g (2½ oz/⅖ cup) light brown soft sugar
25 g (⅘ oz) unsalted butter

FOR THE PLUM CRUMBLE TOPPING

60 g (2 oz) unsalted butter, cubed and chilled
100 g (3½ oz/⅘ cup) plain (all-purpose) flour
60 g (2 oz/⅓ cup) light brown soft sugar
pinch of salt

FOR THE APPLE PIE PASTRY

250 g (9 oz/2 cups) plain (all-purpose) flour, plus extra for dusting
125 g (4 oz) unsalted butter, cubed and chilled
pinch of salt
3–4 tablespoons ice-cold water
1 large (US – extra large) egg, beaten

FOR THE APPLE PIE FILLING

8 apples, peeled, cored and chopped into 1 cm (½ in) cubes
3 tablespoons caster (superfine) sugar
25 g (1 oz) unsalted butter
1 teaspoon ground cinnamon
1 tablespoon water

FOR THE PLUM CRUMBLE

Preheat the oven to 180°C (350°F/gas mark 4). Make the crumble filling by heating all the ingredients in a large saucepan with a lid over a moderate heat. Stir or shake the pan occasionally, for 15 minutes, or until the fruit has softened but can still hold its shape. Then, remove the lid and set the pan aside to allow the filling to fully cool.

To make the crumble topping, place the butter and flour in the bowl of a food processor and process for 20 seconds, or until the mixture looks like breadcrumbs. Stir in the sugar and salt.

Divide the fruit and topping between 4 jars. Bake for 20 minutes, or until golden brown. Let them fully cool before adding the jar lids.

FOR THE APPLE PIE

To make the pastry, mix the flour, butter and salt using a food processor and process for 20 seconds, or until the mixture looks like breadcrumbs. Add the cold water and process again until the mixture forms a ball. Turn the dough out of the bowl, wrap in clingfilm and chill for 30 minutes.

To make the filling, place all the ingredients into a large saucepan with a lid. Bring to the boil and then simmer over a low heat, shaking the pan occasionally. Cook for 10 minutes, or until the apple is soft but still holds its shape. Remove the lid and set aside to allow the filling to fully cool.

Preheat the oven to 180°C (350°F/gas mark 4). Remove your pastry from the fridge and roll it out as thin as possible on a floured surface. Using a sharp knife and jar as a guide, cut out 4 circles to fit the bottom of each jar, and 4 rectangles to line the sides of each jar. Line the jars with the pastry, making sure that all seams are pressed together. Divide the filling between the pastry-lined jars, leaving a 5 mm (¼ inch) gap at the top to attach the lid. Brush the tops of the pastry with the beaten egg, ready for the lids to be placed on.

Roll out the remaining pastry and cut strips for a lattice topping to fit the tops of the jars. Arrange your pastry lids on top of the pies, and seal each pie by pressing the edges of the lid down with a fork. Trim off any excess pastry around the sides so that the jar lid can still be screwed on later. Brush the pastry tops with the remaining egg and bake for 20 minutes, or until golden brown. Let the pies fully cool before adding the jar lids. Store in the fridge for up to 3 days.

CURRANT
SCONES

Scones are one of the first things that I ever learned to bake. They are really simple to make and freshly baked scones are just as delicious buttered for breakfast as they are for enjoying at tea time. Tuck them into a vintage tin and pair them with your favourite jam to make a decorative foodie gift.

MAKES 20

200 g (7 oz/1⅗ cups) plain (all-purpose) flour, plus extra for dusting
1½ teaspoons baking powder
½ teaspoon salt
50 g (2 oz) unsalted butter, cubed and chilled
25 g (1 oz) caster (superfine) sugar
50 g (2 oz) currants
125 ml (4 fl oz) milk, plus extra for glazing

Preheat the oven to 200°C (400°F/gas mark 6), and line a baking tray with baking paper.

Place the flour, baking powder, salt and butter in a bowl and rub together until the mixture looks like breadcrumbs. Add the sugar and currants, then mix to combine. Add the milk and stir to form a soft dough.

Turn the dough out onto a floured surface and knead briefly. Roll out the dough until it is 2 cm (¾ in) thick, then cut out circles using a 4 cm (⅗ in) crinkle cutter. Keep re-rolling and cutting out the dough until it is all used up. Place the scones on the tray and brush with a little milk. Bake for 7–10 minutes, or until golden brown.

Give and eat the scones as soon as possible or store in a tin or airtight container for up to 3 days.

BISCUITS & COOKIES

BLACKCURRANT & VANILLA
LINZER COOKIES

Linzer cookies are usually almond flavoured and sandwiched with raspberry jam. This recipe plays around with that tradition and is inspired by trips to the Czech Republic, where there are always lots of interestingly shaped homemade cookies just waiting to be eaten at Christmas time. These buttery, vanilla-flecked cookies go perfectly with the sweet blackcurrant jam filling. Wrap them in a blackcurrant-hued tissue paper tied with string or ribbon to give as gifts.

MAKES 24

250 g (9 oz) unsalted butter
125 g (4 oz/½ cup) caster
   (superfine) sugar
½ vanilla pod, split lengthways,
   seeds scraped out
300 g (10½ oz/2⅖ cups)
   plain (all-purpose) flour, plus extra
   for dusting
¼ teaspoon salt
120 g (4 oz) blackcurrant jam (jelly)
icing (confectioner's) sugar
   for dusting

Preheat the oven to 170°C (340°F/gas mark 3) and line 2 baking trays with baking paper.

Using a food processor with the beater attachment, mix the butter, sugar and seeds from the vanilla pod until they are smooth and combined. Into a clean bowl sift the flour and salt, then gradually add to the butter mixture, beating in the food processor until the ingredients are just combined.

Turn the dough out onto a floured surface and knead briefly until the dough is smooth. Wrap half of the dough in clingfilm and set it aside. Lay some baking paper on the work surface and roll the other half of the dough out to a thickness of 3–4 mm (⅕ in) onto it. Then, chill the rolled-out dough in the freezer for 10 minutes. (Chilling the dough will make it easier to cut out the circles, see below.)

Remove the dough from the freezer and cut out circles from the dough using a 6 cm (2⅖ in) crinkle cutter. Cut out holes in half of the circles using a 2 cm (¾ in) plain cutter. Transfer all of the circles to the lined baking trays and chill in the freezer for a further 10 minutes – this helps the cookies to keep their shape. Then, bake in the oven for 6–8 minutes, until the biscuits are firm but still pale.

Allow the cookies to cool on a wire rack, and repeat with the remaining cookie dough.

To finish, dab half a teaspoon of jam into the middle of each circle, and place one of the cut-out circles on top to create a cookie sandwich effect. Dust with icing sugar. Store in a tin or an airtight container for up to a week.

BLACK & WHITE COOKIES

These iced trEATs are inspired by another one of my favourite places to visit – New York. They appear in delis and bakeries, where they are often more cake-like than my cookie-based version. Let the glaze set on these for several hours before you wrap them up as presents, and wait to see which side the recipient bites into first. See the picture of them on page 41.

MAKES **24**

FOR THE COOKIES
125 g (4 oz) unsalted butter
125 g (4 oz/½ cup) caster (superfine) sugar
1 large (US – extra large) egg
½ teaspoon vanilla extract
grated zest of 1 lemon
250 g (9 oz/2 cups) plain (all-purpose) flour, plus extra for dusting
½ teaspoon baking powder
pinch of salt

FOR THE GLAZE
½ teaspoon vanilla extract
400 g (14 oz/3⅕ cups) icing (confectioner's) sugar
3–4 tablespoons water
50 g (2 oz) cocoa powder

Preheat the oven to 180°C (350°F/gas mark 4), and line 2 baking trays with baking paper.

Using a food processor with the beater attachment, mix the butter and sugar in a bowl until the mixture is pale and fluffy. Add the egg and mix well to combine, then add the vanilla and lemon zest.

Stir together the flour, baking powder and salt in a clean bowl. Gradually, add this flour mixture to the butter mixture in the food processor, mixing until it is just combined.

Turn the dough out onto a floured surface and knead briefly until the dough is smooth. Wrap half of the dough in clingfilm and set aside. Roll the other half of the dough out to a thickness of 4–5 mm (¼ in).

Cut out circles using a 7 cm (2⅘ in) plain cutter and transfer the circles to one of the baking trays. Repeat with the remaining dough and then chill the cookies in the freezer for 10 minutes – this helps them to keep their shape. Bake in the oven for 10–12 minutes, until firm but still pale.

Allow the cookies to cool on a wire rack.

To make the glaze, whisk together the vanilla extract, half of the icing sugar and half of the water, until it's a smooth paste. In a clean bowl, whisk the remaining icing sugar and water, plus the cocoa powder, until smooth.

Using a palate knife, glaze one half of the top of each cookie with the vanilla glaze, and the other half with the cocoa glaze.

Allow to fully set on a wire rack. Store in a tin or an airtight container for up to 2 weeks.

SPICED PUMPKIN CAKES

These are spiced like pumpkin pie and are great for Halloween parties, or as a spookily seasonal bite-sized trEAT to share. Pumpkin purée can be bought in tins from most big supermarkets, so there's no need to make your own. See the picture of them on page 44.

MAKES 24

FOR THE CAKES
60 g (2 oz) unsalted butter
75 g (2½ oz/⅖ cup) light brown soft sugar
1 large (US – extra large) egg
150 g (5 oz) pumpkin purée
½ teaspoon vanilla extract
150 g (5 oz/1⅕ cups) plain (all-purpose) flour
2 teaspoons baking powder
½ teaspoon ground cinnamon
½ teaspoon ground ginger
pinch of ground nutmeg
¼ teaspoon salt

FOR THE CREAM-CHEESE FROSTING
60 g (2 oz) full-fat cream cheese, chilled
120 g (4 oz/1 cup) golden icing (confectioner's) sugar
pumpkin seeds to decorate

Preheat the oven to 170°C (340°F/gas mark 3). Line a 24-hole mini muffin tin with squares of baking paper or mini cupcake cases.

Melt the butter in a saucepan over a low heat, then allow to cool. Using a food processor with the beater attachment, beat the butter and sugar until combined. Add the egg, pumpkin purée and vanilla extract and mix well.

Into a clean bowl sift the flour, baking powder, spices and salt, and stir to combine. Gradually add the flour mixture to the butter mixture in the food processor, and mix until the ingredients are well combined. Scrape down the sides of the bowl to make sure that all of the ingredients are well incorporated.

Divide the mixture between the cake cases until each case is two-thirds full. Bake in the oven for 12–15 minutes, or until a skewer inserted into one of the cakes comes out clean.

Set the cakes aside to cool in the pan for 2 minutes, before turning out onto a wire rack to cool completely.

To make the cream-cheese frosting, use a food processor with the beater attachment to mix the icing sugar and cream cheese until it forms a smooth mixture. Transfer the frosting to a piping bag with the end cut off, and pipe small amounts of frosting onto the cooled cakes. Finally, decorate with the pumpkin seeds. Though best eaten fresh, you can store the cakes in a tin or an airtight container in the fridge for up to 3 days. Serve at room temperature.

GINGERBREAD
BATS

Bats are my favourite Halloween mascots, and these Gingerbread Bats make a tasty pairing with the Pumpkin Cakes for a Halloween hamper to share with friends. These cookies use the same base as the Mini Gingerbread Houses on page 53. Once you've tried out the recipe for Halloween, why not make some more in the form of festive, edible decorations for Christmas?

Makes 30 bats

FOR THE GINGERBREAD
See page 53

FOR THE DECORATION
250 g (9 oz) Instant Royal Icing sugar (see page 114 for stockists)
2–3 tablespoons water
a few drops of black food colouring

To make your gingerbread dough, follow the recipe on page 53. Chill your dough in the fridge for at least 2 hours to allow it to rest.

Once your dough is fully chilled, preheat the oven to 170°C (340°F/ gas mark 3) and line 2 baking trays with baking paper.

Put one disc in the freezer while you roll out the dough of the other disc to 4–5 mm (¼ in) thick on a floured surface. Cut out bat shapes using a cookie cutter, or make your own cardboard template and use a sharp knife to cut around it. Transfer your bats to the baking trays and chill in the freezer for 10 minutes. Bake in the oven for 8–10 minutes, or until the edges of the shapes are firm. Fully cool on a wire rack. Repeat with the remaining dough.

Using a food processor with the whisk attachment, whisk the Instant Royal Icing sugar with the water for 5 minutes to create a smooth paste that is thick enough to pipe with. Place a small amount of the white icing in a bowl for the bat eyes. Cover and set aside.

Add the black food colouring to the remaining icing and mix well in the with a spatula. Transfer the black icing to a piping bag and snip a small amount off the end. Pipe a black outline on all of the bat shapes. Reserve a small amount of the remaining black icing in the bag for the bat eyes.

Thin out the remaining black icing with some more water to give it a runnier consistency, then, with a teaspoon, use it to fill in the bat outlines.

Allow the icing on your gingerbread bats to set for at least 2 hours, then ice the bat eyes using the remaining white and black icing. Store in a tin or an airtight container for up to 2 weeks.

CHOCOLATE CHIP COOKIES

These chocolate chip cookies are classically crisp on the outside and gratifyingly chewy on the inside. Make this recipe into an easy DIY gift by layering up the ingredients in a 750 ml (25 fl oz) capacity storage jar: place the flour mixture at the bottom followed by layers of the sugars and chocolate. Hand-write a label with instructions to add 150 g (5 oz) of softened, unsalted butter and 1 egg. Personalise by swapping out the dark chocolate for a mix of white chocolate and crushed hazelnuts, cinnamon and raisin, or anything that takes your fancy.

MAKES 36

150 g (5 oz) unsalted butter
100 g (3½ oz/⅖ cup)
  caster (superfine) sugar
150 g (5 oz/⅘ cup) light brown
  soft sugar
1 large (US – extra large) egg
200 g (7 oz) dark chocolate,
  roughly chopped
250 g (9 oz/2 cups) plain
  (all-purpose) flour
1 teaspoon bicarbonate of soda
½ teaspoon sea salt

Using a food processor with the beater attachment, mix the butter and sugars until the mixture is pale and fluffy. Add the egg and mix well to combine, then add the chocolate.

Into a clean bowl sift the flour, bicarbonate of soda and salt, and stir to combine. Gradually add the flour mixture to the butter mixture, mixing with the food processor until it is just combined. Cover the bowl and chill for at least 2 hours in the fridge.

When your cookie dough is fully chilled, preheat the oven to 170°C (340°F/gas mark 3). Line 2 baking trays with baking paper. Using a small ice-cream scoop or teaspoon, scoop out small amounts of the dough (about 20 g/¾ oz), roll into balls with your hands and place on the baking trays 5 cm (2 in) apart – the cookies will flatten out as they bake. It should be possible to fit nine cookies on each tray, so you will need to work in two batches.

Bake in the oven for 8 minutes, or until just firm and golden at the edges. Leave the cookies to cool on the baking trays for 2–3 minutes before transferring the cookies, on the baking paper, to fully cool on a wire rack.

Repeat with the rest of the dough, or freeze the remaining dough for up to a month. Store the baked cookies in a tin or an airtight container for up to 2 weeks.

TINY LEMON MERINGUE PIE COOKIES

The lemon-flavoured base and royal-icing peaks of these cookies make them like tiny bites of lemon meringue pie. The royal icing sets hard so that you can pile up the cookies and package them in a labelled jar or cellophane bag without worrying about them getting squashed. Give these cookies as a gift alongside a new pie tin and a favourite recipe for lemon meringue pie as an extra-special trEAT.

MAKES 100

FOR THE BISCUITS

60 g (2 oz) unsalted butter
60 g (2 oz/¼ cup) caster (superfine) sugar
1 large (US – extra large) egg yolk
grated zest of 1 lemon
125 g (4 oz/1 cup) plain (all-purpose) flour, plus extra for dusting
¼ teaspoon baking powder
pinch of salt

FOR THE 'MERINGUE' ICING

200 g (7 oz) Instant Royal Icing sugar (see page 114 for stockists)
2–3 tablespoons water
yellow nonpareils or sprinkles to decorate

Preheat the oven to 170°C (340°F/gas mark 3), and line 2 baking trays with baking paper.

Using a food processor with the beater attachment, mix the butter and sugar until the mixture is pale and fluffy. Add the egg and mix well to combine, then add the lemon zest.

Into a clean bowl sift the flour, baking powder and salt and stir to combine. Gradually add the flour mixture to the butter mixture, mixing with the food processor until it is just combined.

Turn the dough out onto a floured surface and knead briefly until smooth. Roll the dough out onto some baking paper until it is 3–4 mm (⅕ in) thick, then chill it in the freezer for 10 minutes.

Remove the dough from the freezer and cut out 2 cm (¾ in) circles using a fluted cutter. Transfer these to the lined baking tray and chill in the freezer for a further 10 minutes – this helps the cookies to keep their shape as they bake. Bake in the oven for 3–5 minutes, until firm but still pale.

Allow the cookies to cool on a wire rack.

To make the 'meringue' icing, mix the Instant Royal Icing sugar with the water to form a smooth paste for piping. Transfer the icing into a piping bag fitted with a 1M (star) icing tip. Ice a single peak on each cooled cookie and sprinkle with the yellow nonpareils to decorate. Allow to set hard before packaging up. Store in a tin or an airtight container for up to 2 weeks.

LIBERTY-PRINT INSPIRED CHOCOLATE HEARTS

Liberty is one of my favourite shops in London for gifts – edible or otherwise. These Liberty-fabric inspired biscuits look like they've been hand-painted, but are actually decorated using chocolate transfer paper. Try experimenting with different patterns and cookie cutters. Wrap a batch of these in transparent paper and tie with ribbon for a pretty and personal Valentine's or Mother's Day gift.

MAKES 24 (DEPENDING ON THE SIZE OF YOUR CUTTERS)

FOR THE CHOCOLATE COOKIES
125 g (4 oz) unsalted butter
125 g (4 oz/½ cup) caster (superfine) sugar
1 large (US – extra large) egg
½ teaspoon vanilla extract
200 g (7 oz/1⅗ cups) plain (all-purpose) flour, plus extra for dusting
50 g (2 oz) cocoa powder
½ teaspoon baking powder
pinch of salt

FOR THE DECORATION
200 g (7 oz) white chocolate, chopped
1 A3 chocolate transfer paper with a floral print design

Preheat the oven to 170°C (340°F/gas mark 3) and line 2 baking trays with baking paper. Using a food processor with the beater attachment, mix the butter and sugar until the mixture is pale and fluffy. Add the egg and mix well to combine, then add the vanilla extract.

Into a clean bowl sift the flour, cocoa, baking powder and salt. Gradually add this flour mixture to the butter mixture, mixing with the food processor until just combined.

Turn the dough out onto a floured surface and knead briefly until the dough is smooth. Wrap half of the dough in clingfilm and set aside. Roll the other half of the dough out onto a floured surface until it is 3–4 mm (⅕ in) thick. Then, cut out heart shapes using a heart cutter in one or two different sizes. Transfer the shapes to one of the baking trays. Repeat with the remaining dough and chill in the freezer for 10 minutes (this helps the cookies to keep their shape). Bake in the oven for 8–12 minutes (depending on the size of your shapes), until firm. Allow the cookies to cool on a wire rack.

To make the decoration, melt the white chocolate in a glass bowl over a saucepan of simmering water, ensuring that the water doesn't touch the bottom of the bowl. Stir until the chocolate is almost melted, then remove the pan from the heat. Remove the bowl from the saucepan, and continue to stir until the chocolate is completely melted. Then, allow it to cool slightly.

Place the sheets of transfer paper design-side up on 2 baking trays. Pour the melted chocolate onto the transfer paper and spread evenly over the sheet with a palate knife until it is 1–2 mm (⅛ in) thick. Chill the chocolate in the fridge for 10 minutes, or until firm (but not completely set).

Press the heart cutters through the chocolate to the transfer paper. Return the baking trays to the fridge to allow the chocolate to fully set. Turn the chocolate over so that the design side is facing up, then carefully peel away the transfer paper to reveal the floral design, and push out the heart shapes. Set aside any leftover white chocolate.

To attach the chocolate paper to the cookies, melt the white chocolate that was left over after pushing out the heart shapes. Place a small amount of melted chocolate on each cookie to act as a glue, and place the chocolate hearts on top. Set aside to fully set. Store in a tin or an airtight container for up to 2 weeks.

MINI GINGERBREAD HOUSES

These mini houses are surprisingly sturdy once they're put together. Seek out gift bags that have a base to keep the houses upright, and decorate the gingerbread as elaborately or as simply as you like. I love the simple white-with-a-pop-of-red look. A sparkle of white, edible glitter would work really well too.

MAKES 10 HOUSES

FOR THE GINGERBREAD
100 g (3½ oz) unsalted butter
75 g (2½ oz) treacle
75 g (2½ oz) golden syrup
75 g (2½ oz/⅖ cup) dark brown soft sugar
450 g (1 lb/3⅗ cups) plain (all-purpose) flour, plus extra for dusting
1 teaspoon baking powder
1 teaspoon salt
½ teaspoon ground cloves
2 teaspoons ground ginger
1 teaspoon ground cinnamon
pinch of ground nutmeg
pinch of ground black pepper
1 large (US – extra large) egg yolk
1 tablespoon grated fresh ginger

FOR THE ASSEMBLY AND DECORATION
500 g (1 lb 2 oz) Instant Royal Icing sugar (see page 114 for stockists)
4–5 tablespoons water
sprinkles and white sanding sugar to decorate

To make the gingerbread, heat the butter, treacle, golden syrup and sugar in a large saucepan over a medium heat. Stir until the butter has melted and all of the ingredients are well combined. Remove from the heat and set aside to cool.

Into a clean bowl sift the flour, baking powder, salt, cloves, ginger, cinnamon, nutmeg and pepper, and stir to combine. Once the butter mixture has cooled, add the egg yolk and fresh ginger to it, mixing well. Then, fold in the flour mixture to form a dough.

Turn the dough out onto a floured surface and knead briefly until smooth. Split into two discs and wrap each one with clingfilm. Chill them in the fridge for at least 2 hours to allow the dough to rest. Now make your house templates: trace the shapes on page 111 onto some cardboard and label each one accordingly.

Once your dough is fully chilled, preheat the oven to 170°C (340°F/ gas mark 3) and line 2 baking trays with baking paper. One disc at a time, roll out the dough on a floured surface to 4–5 mm (¼ in) thick. Next, place your templates on top of the dough and cut out each shape (sides, ends and roof) with a sharp knife for each house.

Transfer your house shapes to the trays and chill in the freezer for 10 minutes. Bake in the oven for 8 minutes, or until the edges of the shapes are firm. Before the gingerbread cools, place the templates back on top of the shapes and trim any edges that may have spread while baking.

Allow the shapes to cool on a wire rack and bake the remaining gingerbread pieces.

Once your gingerbread has completely cooled, start assembling the houses. To make your icing glue, use a food processor with the whisk attachment and whisk the Instant Royal Icing sugar with the water for 5 minutes. This will create a paste that is thick enough to pipe with. Transfer to a piping bag and snip a small amount off of the end. To assemble the houses, start with the ends and sides, using plenty of icing to glue it all together, then add the roof. Allow the icing to set before decorating with more icing and lots of sprinkles. Store in a tin or an airtight container for up to 2 weeks.

NEAPOLITAN SANDWICH COOKIES

I love the sunny combination of flavours in these cookies, and when stacked one on top of the other they remind me of scoops of ice cream piled up in a cone. Package them up in pastel-coloured boxes, and experiment with different buttercream fillings that combine well with vanilla and chocolate, such as pistachio or chestnut.

MAKES **30**

FOR THE CHOCOLATE COOKIES
125 g (4 oz) unsalted butter
125 g (4 oz/½ cup) caster (superfine) sugar
1 large (US – extra large) egg
½ teaspoon vanilla extract
200 g (7 oz/1⅗ cups) plain (all-purpose) flour, plus extra for dusting
50 g (2 oz) cocoa powder
½ teaspoon baking powder
pinch of salt

FOR THE VANILLA COOKIES
125 g (4 oz) unsalted butter
125 g (4 oz/½ cup) caster (superfine) sugar
1 large (US – extra large) egg
1 teaspoon vanilla extract
250 g (9 oz/2 cups) plain (all-purpose) flour
½ teaspoon baking powder
pinch of salt

FOR THE STRAWBERRY BUTTERCREAM
125 g (4 oz) unsalted butter
125 g (4 oz/1 cup) icing (confectioner's) sugar
1–2 teaspoons milk
2 tablespoons strawberry jam (jelly)

Preheat the oven to 170°C (340°F/gas mark 3), and line 2 baking trays with baking paper.

To make the chocolate cookies, use a food processor with the beater attachment to mix the butter and sugar until the mixture is pale and fluffy. Add the egg and mix well to combine, then add the vanilla.

Into a clean bowl sift the flour, cocoa, baking powder and salt, and stir to combine. Add this flour mixture to the butter mixture in the food processor, mixing until it is all just combined. Turn the dough out onto a floured surface and knead briefly until smooth.

To make the vanilla cookies, use a food processor with the beater attachment to mix the butter and sugar until the mixture is pale and fluffy. Add the egg and mix well to combine, then add the vanilla.

Into a clean bowl sift the flour, baking powder and salt, and stir to combine. Add this flour mixture to the butter mixture in the food processor, mixing until just combined. Turn the dough out onto a floured surface and knead briefly until smooth.

Roll out half of the chocolate dough and half of the vanilla dough side by side (so that they are an identical thickness) until they are 5 mm (¼ in) thick. Cut out circles using a 3.5 cm (1⅖ in) cutter. Transfer the different flavoured shapes to one of the baking trays, repeat with the remaining dough and then chill both trays with the circles in the freezer for 10 minutes (this helps the cookies to keep their shape). Bake in the oven for 8 minutes, until firm.

Cool on a wire rack.

To make the strawberry buttercream, use a food processor with the beater attachment to beat the butter, icing sugar and milk for 4–5 minutes, or until the mixture is pale and creamy. Add the strawberry jam and mix well to combine. Transfer the buttercream to a piping bag, snip the end and pipe a small amount onto each cooled vanilla cookie. Top with the chocolate cookies and press together. Store in the fridge in an airtight container for up to a week.

S'MORES

S'mores, short for 'some more', are an American campfire trEAT that take toasted marshmallows up a notch by pairing them with chocolate and sandwiching them between two cookies. The spelt flour and brown sugar make these cookies work really well with the sweet marshmallow and chocolate filling. Package them into little kits in vintage-style campfire-friendly mugs (even if there isn't a campfire in sight!)

MAKES 20

FOR THE COOKIES
175 g (6 oz) unsalted butter
75 g (2 ½ oz/⅖ cup) light brown soft sugar
3 tablespoons golden syrup
1 teaspoon vanilla extract
450 g (1 lb, 3⅗ cups) plain (all-purpose) spelt flour, plus extra for dusting
1 teaspoon ground cinnamon
1 teaspoon baking powder
½ teaspoon salt

FOR THE TOPPING
2 tablespoons light brown soft sugar
1 teaspoon ground cinnamon

FOR THE FILLING
100 g (3½ oz) dark or milk chocolate, roughly chopped
20 marshmallows, halved

Preheat the oven to 180°C (350°F/gas mark 4) and line 2 baking trays with baking paper.

Using a food processor with the beater attachment, mix the butter, sugar and golden syrup until the mixture is pale and fluffy, then add the vanilla.

Into a clean bowl sift the flour, cinnamon, baking powder and salt, and stir to combine. Gradually add this flour mixture to the butter mixture in the food processor, and mix until a dough forms. Split the dough into 2 halves and wrap one half in clingfilm and set aside.

Roll out the other half of the dough onto a floured surface to 3 mm (⅛ in) thick. Next, cut the dough into rectangles measuring 5 × 8 cm (2 × 3⅛ in). Transfer the rectangles to the baking trays and make a pattern on the top using a fork or lollipop stick. Sprinkle the rectangles with the sugar and cinnamon topping, then chill them in the freezer for 10 minutes. Bake for 7–8 minutes in batches in the oven, until the cookies are firm and golden brown.

Allow the cookies to fully cool on a wire rack, and repeat with the remaining dough.

To assemble the s'mores, work in batches of 4: place 4 cookies at a time face-side down on a lined baking tray. Place 2 marshmallow halves on each cookie. Heat them under a medium grill for a few seconds, until the marshmallow starts to melt, then remove them from the heat, sprinkle some chopped chocolate over the top, and sandwich each one by pressing another cookie on top.

Alternatively, toast your marshmallows on a campfire and sandwich along with a chunk of chocolate between 2 cookies. Store the cookies in a tin or an airtight container for up to 2 weeks. Eat assembled s'mores straight away.

WHITE-CHOCOLATE-DIPPED PISTACHIO & APRICOT COOKIES

The apricots in these cookies give them a lovely chewy texture. Try presenting these in a vintage tin with blues or greens to complement the colour of the chopped pistachios.

MAKES 48

FOR THE COOKIES
225 g (8 oz) unsalted butter
225 g (8 oz/1 cup) caster
  (superfine) sugar
1 large (US – extra large) egg
2 teaspoons vanilla extract
450 g (1 lb/3⅗ cups) plain
  (all-purpose) flour, plus
  extra for dusting
¾ teaspoon baking powder
½ teaspoon salt
150 g (5 oz) dried apricots,
  roughly chopped
150 g (5 oz) pistachios, roughly
  chopped

FOR THE DECORATION
200 g (7 oz) white chocolate
50 g (2 oz) pistachios, roughly
  chopped

Preheat the oven to 170°C (340°F/gas mark 3) and line 2 baking trays with baking paper.

Using a food processor with the beater attachment, mix the butter and sugar until the mixture is pale and fluffy. Add the egg and mix well to combine, then add the vanilla.

Into a clean bowl sift the flour, baking powder and salt, and stir to combine. Add half of this flour mixture to the butter mixture in the food processor, mixing until just incorporated. Add the apricots and pistachios and mix to combine, then add the remaining flour mixture and mix until it is just combined.

Turn the dough out onto a floured surface and knead briefly until smooth. Roll out the dough to 5 mm (¼ in) thick. Cut out circles using a 6 cm (2⅖ in) cutter.

Working in batches, to fit in your freezer and oven, transfer the shapes to the baking tray and chill in the freezer for 10 minutes. Then bake in the oven for 8–10 minutes, until firm.

Allow to cool on a wire rack, and repeat with the remaining dough.

While your cookies are cooling, you can prepare the decoration: to make the white-chocolate coating, melt the chocolate in a glass bowl over a saucepan of simmering water, ensuring that the water doesn't touch the bottom of the bowl. Stir until the chocolate is almost melted, then remove the pan from the heat. Remove the glass bowl from the saucepan to ensure that the chocolate doesn't become overheated, and continue to stir until the chocolate is completely melted, then allow to cool slightly.

Line 2 baking trays with baking paper. Dip each cookie halfway into the melted chocolate, tap off the excess and place on a tray. Sprinkle some chopped pistachios over the top, and leave to fully set. Store in a tin or an airtight container for up to 2 weeks.

SAVOURY trEATs

SAVOURY FIG & GOAT'S CHEESE CAKES

These savoury trEATs look so pretty with a sprig of rosemary on the top. Try throwing a few olives or capers into the mix, or swap the goat's cheese for a soft blue cheese.

MAKES 8

250 g (9 oz/2 cups) plain
  (all-purpose) flour
2 teaspoons baking powder
½ teaspoon salt
½ teaspoon ground black
  pepper
2 large (US – extra large) eggs
150 ml (5 fl oz) milk
150 g (5 oz) unsalted butter,
  melted and cooled
2 tablespoons finely chopped
  fresh rosemary, plus extra sprigs
  for decorating
100 g (3½ oz) goat's cheese,
  cubed
3 ripe figs, quartered

Preheat the oven to 180°C (350°F/gas mark 4). Place 8 mini cardboard loaf cases on a baking tray.

Into a clean bowl sift the flour, baking powder, salt and pepper, and stir to combine.

In a clean bowl, whisk together the eggs, milk and butter in a bowl. Gradually add the egg mixture to the flour mixture, whisking until just combined, then add the chopped rosemary.

Divide the batter between the loaf cases until each case is half full. Press the goat's cheese and figs into the top of each cake. Bake in the oven for 20 minutes, or until a skewer inserted into one of the cakes comes out clean.

Cool on a wire rack. Once cool, decorate with the extra sprigs of rosemary. Though best eaten fresh, you can store the cakes in a tin or an airtight container in the fridge for up to 3 days. Serve at room temperature.

OATCAKES WITH PINK PEPPERCORNS

The pink peppercorns in these oatcakes gives them a pretty pop of colour as well as adding a bit of heat. Package the oatcakes up with some artisan cheese, and give them to your favourite midnight snacker as a gift, or keep them all to yourself.

MAKES 30

75 g (2½ oz) unsalted butter
3 tablespoons boiling water
200 g (7 oz/1 cup) oatmeal
50 g (2 oz/⅖ cup) plain
   (all-purpose) flour, plus extra
   for dusting
½ teaspoon salt
2–3 teaspoons pink peppercorns,
   crushed

Preheat the oven to 180°C (350°F/gas mark 4), and line 2 baking trays with baking paper.

Heat the butter in a large saucepan over a low heat until it is melted, then add the boiling water and mix together.

In a clean bowl, mix the oatmeal, flour, salt and peppercorns to combine. Add this flour mixture to the butter and mix together. Turn out the mixture onto a floured surface, and squash the mixture together with your hands to form a dough. Working quickly (the mixture becomes dry as it cools), roll out the dough to a 4–5 mm (¼ in) thickness and cut out circles with a 5 cm (2 in) cutter. Transfer the circles to the prepared baking trays, and bake in the oven for 12–15 minutes, or until firm.

Allow the oatcakes to fully cool on the trays. Store in a tin or an airtight container for up to 2 weeks.

CHEESE STRAWS WITH CARAWAY SEEDS

These cheese straws are like savoury fingers of shortbread and make a flavoursome pairing with cold beer. Bundle them in greaseproof paper to present them as a gift.

MAKES ABOUT 50

300 g (10½ oz) mature
   Cheddar, grated
100 g (3½ oz) butter, cubed
   and chilled
200 g (7 oz/1⅗ cups) plain
   (all-purpose) flour, plus extra
   for dusting
good pinch of salt
1 large (US – extra large) egg yolk
1 tablespoon caraway seeds

Preheat the oven to 180°C (350°F/gas mark 4), and line 2 baking trays with baking paper.

Place the cheese, butter, flour, salt and egg yolk into the bowl of a food processor, and process briefly with the beater attachment to form a dough. Turn the dough out onto a floured surface and scatter the caraway seeds over it. Knead the dough briefly until it is smooth, then roll out the dough and cut long, 2-cm- (¾-in-) wide strips with a pizza wheel or sharp knife.

Transfer the dough strips to the prepared trays and chill them in the freezer for 10 minutes (this helps the straws to keep their shape). Bake in the oven for 8 minutes, or until golden brown.

Allow to fully cool on a wire rack, then store in a tin or an airtight container for up to a week.

SMOKED PAPRIKA ALMONDS

A sweet, salty, smoky and addictive combination, these spiced almonds are perfect for drinks parties. Try the recipe with other nuts, such as pecans or walnuts, too, and vary the amount of chilli powder you use, depending on how much heat you like. Package them into jars or small cellophane bags tied with string to give as nutty gifts.

Fills 2 × 250 ml (8½ fl oz) jars

300 g (10½ oz) whole almonds
1 tablespoon caster (superfine) sugar
1 tablespoon smoked paprika
1 teaspoon ground cinnamon
¼ teaspoon chilli powder
2 teaspoons sea salt

FOR THE SUGAR SYRUP
100 g (3½ oz/⅖ cup) caster (superfine) sugar
100 ml (3½ fl oz) water

Preheat the oven to 150°C (300°F/gas mark 2), and line a baking tray with baking paper.

Spread the almonds on the tray and bake for 10 minutes (leave the oven on when you remove the almonds). Meanwhile, combine the sugar, spices and salt in a large bowl and set aside.

To make the sugar syrup, heat the sugar and water in a small saucepan over a medium heat, and stir until the sugar has dissolved. Then, remove the saucepan from the heat, add the baked almonds, and stir to combine.

Drain the sugar syrup by pouring the mixture through a sieve (keep the syrup if you're making another batch). Then, toss the nuts in the sugar, spice and salt mixture.

Spread the nuts evenly on the lined tray, return the tray to the oven and bake for another 5–10 minutes, or until golden brown.

Set aside to fully cool. Store in a tin or an airtight container for up to 2 weeks.

PRETZELS

These savoury snacks start off as pizza dough, but the poaching transforms them into glossy, chewy pretzels. Package them in paper bags, as airtight containers don't agree with them. Try alternative seeds for sprinkling, such as poppy or caraway seeds, depending on what you've got in the cupboard. They're also great with a dash of mild mustard on the side.

MAKES 12

350 g (12 oz/2⅖ cups) plain
   (all-purpose) flour
7 g (¼ oz) sachet of dried yeast
½ teaspoon salt
2 teaspoons caster (superfine) sugar
2 tablespoons olive oil, plus extra
   for greasing
200 ml (7 fl oz) warm water
3 tablespoons baking powder
1 large (US – extra large) egg,
   beaten
sesame seeds for sprinkling

To make the dough, combine the flour, yeast, salt and sugar in a large bowl, then add the oil and warm water, and combine to form a ball. Turn the dough out onto a floured surface and knead for 5–10 minutes until it is smooth. Transfer the mixture to an oiled bowl, cover with clingfilm and leave to rise for 1 hour, or until it has doubled in size.

Preheat the oven to 200°C (400°F/gas mark 6).

To make the pretzel shapes, take 45 g (2 oz) of dough at a time, and roll into 50 cm (20 in) lengths. Twist into a pretzel shape and set aside.

Put some kitchen paper on a plate and set aside, ready for transferring your pretzels to. Fill a frying pan with water, stir in the baking powder, and bring it to a simmer. Add the pretzels to the water in two batches, simmering each batch for 30 seconds on each side. Using tongs or a slotted spoon, remove the poached pretzels from the frying pan and place onto the kitchen paper.

Lightly oil 2 baking trays. Transfer the pretzels to the trays, and brush with the beaten egg. Sprinkle the pretzels with the sesame seeds and bake in the oven for 10–12 minutes, until golden. Though best eaten fresh, you can store the pretzels for up to 2 days (covered).

INFUSED OILS

These oils are delicious drizzled onto pasta and salad, or used as a dip for bread. The rosemary oil should be kept in the fridge and will keep for a week. The chilli oil can be kept at room temperature and will last for several weeks.

FILLS 2 × 250 ML
(8½ FL OZ) BOTTLES

FOR THE ROSEMARY OIL
250 ml (8½ fl oz) olive oil
5 sprigs of rosemary
pinch of sea salt

FOR THE CHILLI OIL
250 ml (8½ fl oz) olive oil
2 tablespoons chilli flakes, plus
   a few extra
pinch of sea salt

For the rosemary oil, gently heat the olive oil, 4 of the 5 sprigs of rosemary, and salt in a medium saucepan for 4–5 minutes. Remove the saucepan from the heat and allow the oil to fully cool.

Once the oil has cooled, cover it and leave overnight to let the flavours infuse. Then, pour into a clean, sterilised bottle with the remaining rosemary sprig and seal.

For the chilli oil, gently heat the olive oil, chilli flakes and salt in a medium saucepan for 4–5 minutes, until the oil turns slightly red. Remove the saucepan from the heat and allow the oil to fully cool.

Once the oil has cooled, cover it and leave overnight to let the flavours infuse and the oil take on the redness of the chilli. Then, run the oil through a sieve to remove the chilli flakes, pour into a clean, sterilised bottle with a few new flakes and seal.

FLAVOURED SALTS

These little jars of flavoured flaky sea salt are really simple to make. Try sprinkling the flavoured salt onto poached eggs, toss it into popcorn or serve it with homemade potato wedges.

FILLS 3 × 120 ML
(4 FL OZ) JARS

FOR THE SPICY, SMOKED-PAPRIKA SALT
60 g (2 oz) sea salt
2 teaspoons smoked paprika
½ teaspoon chilli powder

FOR THE GARLIC SALT
60 g (2 oz) sea salt
4 teaspoons garlic powder

FOR THE ROSEMARY SALT
60 g (2 oz) sea salt
2 sprigs of rosemary

To make the spicy, smoked-paprika salt and the garlic salt, combine all the ingredients of each recipe into a bowl, then place in a clean, sterilised jar and seal. These flavoured salts will keep at room temperature for several weeks.

To make the rosemary salt, preheat the oven to 200°C (400°F/ gas mark 6). Place one of the rosemary sprigs in a ramekin or small, ovenproof dish and cover with the salt. Bake in the oven for 10 minutes.

Allow the salt to fully cool, then cover and leave to rest at room temperature overnight.

The next morning, remove the baked rosemary and transfer the salt to a clean, sterilised jar. Add the fresh sprig of rosemary and seal. This flavoured salt should be kept in the fridge and will keep for a week.

SWEET trEATs

VIOLET & PEPPERMINT CREAMS

Make these into grown-up trEATs by decorating them with simple sprinkles or crystallised violet petals, and presenting them in glassine chocolate cases. They are beautiful packaged up in an old tin, but you can also layer them up in a cellophane bag, which works well if you want to make a big batch to give as gifts to lots of people.

MAKES **30** OF EITHER FLAVOUR

FOR THE DOUGH
1 large (US – extra large) egg white
250 g (9 oz/2 cups) icing (confectioner's) sugar, plus more for rolling out
1–2 drops violet or peppermint extract

FOR THE CHOCOLATE COATING
100 g (3½ oz) dark chocolate, finely chopped
sprinkles or crystallised violet petals

Line a baking tray with baking paper.

Using a food processor, whisk the egg white until it is foamy. Add the extract and half of the sugar, and whisk to incorporate. Add the remaining sugar and form a soft dough. Use your hands to lightly knead the dough until smooth. Check the flavouring and add more extract if needed. If the dough is too sticky to roll, add some more sugar.

Dust the work surface with icing sugar. Roll out the dough until it is 5–10 mm (¼–½ in) thick. Cut the dough into 3-cm (1-⅕-in) rounds if you are making peppermint creams, and roll the rounds into little balls if you are making violet creams, then transfer to the lined baking tray.

Leave the dough rounds and balls at room temperature for 1 hour, or until set.

To make the coating, heat the chocolate in a glass bowl over a saucepan of simmering water, ensuring that the water doesn't touch the bottom of the bowl. Stir until the chocolate is almost melted, then remove the pan from the heat. Remove the glass bowl from the saucepan to ensure that the chocolate doesn't become overheated, and continue to stir the chocolate until it is completely melted, then set it aside to cool slightly.

Once your basic creams have set and your chocolate has cooled, you can get ready to dip and decorate: line 2 baking trays with baking paper. Stick a cocktail stick into a cream and dip it halfway into the chocolate. Tap off the excess chocolate and transfer it to one of the lined trays. Repeat until all of the creams have been dipped, then decorate: use the sprinkles for a batch of peppermint flavour creams, and a single petal for a batch of violet creams.

Allow the chocolate on your creams to fully set, then transfer them to chocolate cases. Store in cellophane bags, a tin or an airtight container for up to 2 weeks.

WARNING: Uncooked egg whites are not suitable for young children, pregnant women and elderly people.

CANDIED CASHEWS

This is a simple way of adding a crunchy sugar coating to the roasted cashews. Make sure they're completely cooled before you wrap them, and present them in a vintage-style enamel mug.

FILLS 2 × 250 ML
(8½ FL OZ) MUGS OR JARS

250 g (9 oz) raw cashew nuts
100 g (3½ oz/⅖ cup)
   caster (superfine) sugar (plus
   3 tablespoons for sprinkling)
100 ml (3½ fl oz) water
pinch of sea salt

Preheat the oven to 150°C (300°F/gas mark 2) and line a baking tray with baking paper.

Spread the nuts on the tray and bake in the oven for 10 minutes.

Meanwhile, to make the sugar syrup, heat the sugar and water in a saucepan over a medium heat, and stir until the sugar has dissolved. Then, remove the saucepan from the heat, add the baked nuts, and stir to combine.

Drain the sugar syrup by pouring the mixture through a sieve (keep the syrup if you're making another batch). Spread the syrupy cashews evenly on the lined tray, and sprinkle 3 tablespoons of caster sugar and a pinch of sea salt over the top. Return the tray to the oven and bake for another 5–10 minutes, or until the cashews are golden brown.

Allow the cashews to fully cool before wrapping – any trapped humidity will cause the sugar coating to become sticky. Store in cellophane bags, a tin or an airtight container for up to 2 weeks.

CANDIED ORANGE DIPPED IN DARK CHOCOLATE

Candying orange slices brings out their beautiful colour, which makes them perfect for gifts but also great decorations for citrus or chocolate cakes. They're quite a sticky trEAT so however you package them up, always layer them in between squares of baking paper.

MAKES 16 SLICES

2 oranges
500 g (1 lb 2 oz/2¼ cups) caster (superfine) sugar
500 ml (17 fl oz) water
100 g (3½ oz) dark chocolate, finely chopped

Line a baking tray with baking paper.

Slice each orange across the middle into around 8 thin slices. Heat the sugar and water in a large saucepan over a medium heat and bring to a boil – continue boiling until the sugar has dissolved.

Once the sugar has dissolved, place the orange slices into the saucepan and reduce to a simmer. Simmer for 1 hour, or until the orange slices are translucent and the peel is tender. Transfer the orange slices to the lined baking tray and leave to cool and set for several hours, or overnight.

Once the orange slices are cool and dry, line 2 baking trays with baking paper. Heat the chocolate in a glass bowl over a saucepan of simmering water, ensuring that the water doesn't touch the bottom of the bowl. Stir until the chocolate is almost melted, then remove the pan from the heat. Remove the glass bowl from the saucepan to ensure that the chocolate doesn't become overheated, and continue to stir the chocolate until it is completely melted. Allow the chocolate to cool slightly, then dip each orange slice halfway into the chocolate, tap off the excess and transfer to the trays.

Allow the chocolate to set before packaging and wrapping. Store in cellophane bags, a tin or an airtight container in the fridge for up to 3 days.

CHOCOLATE SALAMI

This easy, no-baking-required trEAT can be adapted to suit whatever biscuits or nuts you have in the cupboard. Try a mix of pistachios, pecans and flaked almonds for a seriously nutty result. Wrap your finished 'salami' in baking paper and string to look like the real thing, and slice with a sharp knife to serve.

MAKES ONE SALAMI,
APPROXIMATELY 12 SLICES

100 g (3½ oz) digestive
   or shortbread biscuits
50 g (2 oz) unsalted butter
1 tablespoon golden syrup
30 g (1 oz) cocoa powder
75 g (2½ oz) mixed nuts,
   roughly chopped
icing (confectioner's) sugar
   for dusting

Line a baking tray with a large piece of foil.

Place the biscuits in a freezer bag and crush with the back of a wooden spoon until there is a mixture of crumbs and small pieces.

Heat the butter and golden syrup in a large saucepan over a medium heat until the mixture is completely melted. Remove the pan from the heat, then stir in the cocoa powder and add the crushed biscuits and nuts. Mix until all the ingredients are well combined, then tip the mixture onto the prepared tray. Squash the crumbly mixture into a long salami shape. Wrap the foil around the 'salami' and squeeze everything together with your hands.

Chill the foil-wrapped 'salami' in the fridge for 2 hours, or until firm. Then, unwrap and dust with icing sugar, patting the sugar into the surface for a genuine salami effect.

Wrap your chocolate charcuterie trEAT in baking paper tied with string, and store in the fridge, in an airtight container, for up to a week.

WHITE CHOCOLATE & FRESH BERRY BITES

These bites are super simple and use silicone ice-cube moulds to get that perfect cube shape. Experiment with different berries, depending on the season.

MAKES 18

200 g (7 oz) white chocolate, finely chopped
18 raspberries or blackberries, halved

Heat the chocolate in a glass bowl over a saucepan of simmering water, ensuring that the water doesn't touch the bottom of the bowl. Stir until the chocolate is almost melted, then remove the pan from the heat. Remove the glass bowl from the saucepan to ensure that the chocolate doesn't become overheated, and continue to stir until the chocolate is completely melted.

Allow the chocolate to cool slightly before pouring it into an 18-hole silicone ice-cube tray. Fill each hole with chocolate until it is half full, then carefully press two berry halves into each square. Top up each hole with the remaining chocolate.

Chill the ice-cube tray in the fridge for 2 hours, or until completely firm, and then turn the chocolates out and wrap them in cellophane bags, or store in a tin or an airtight container. Keep them in the fridge and eat within 2–3 days.

SALTED CARAMEL SAUCE

This intensely sweet, salty and buttery caramel takes a bit of practice, but it is well worth mastering. Pour it warm over ice cream, whip it into buttercream or use it to make Brownies (page 14) or Truffles (page 102).

MAKES 1 500-G (1-LB-2-OZ) JAR

250 g (9 oz/1 cup) caster (superfine) sugar
50 g (2 oz) butter, melted
300 ml (10 fl oz) double (thick) cream, warmed
1–2 teaspoons flaky sea salt

Heat the sugar in a large saucepan (a silver-coloured saucepan is best as you need to check the colour of the sugar as it melts) over a medium heat. Once the sugar starts to melt, swirl and push the sugar into the liquid areas of the pan using a wooden spoon, but without stirring. After about 10 minutes, or once the sugar is completely melted and dark amber in colour, remove the saucepan from the heat.

Whisk in the melted butter followed by the warmed cream (be careful, as the mixture can splash up). If the sugar solidifies, return the pan to a medium heat until the mixture is liquid again. Stir in the salt.

Pour the mixture through a sieve to remove any lumps of sugar into a heatproof bowl, and leave to cool before covering and chilling. Keep for up to a week in the fridge.

DIPPED & DECORATED MARSHMALLOWS

Pretty and easy, these dressed-up marshmallows are dipped in candy melts, which come in lots of different colours. If your sweet tooth lends itself more to chocolatey trEATs, you could also try these dipped in white or dark chocolate. Sit them in mini cupcake cases and pack them in layers into a chocolate box or cute tin, layers separated with baking paper, to make an enticing gift.

MAKES 20

400 g (14 oz) candy melts
1–3 tablespoons vegetable oil
20 marshmallows
sprinkles to decorate

Line a baking tray with baking paper.

Melt the candy melts by following the instructions on the packet and stir in the oil until the candy is smooth and runny. Set the candy melts aside to cool slightly.

Once the candy melts have cooled, stick a toothpick into the bottom of the first marshmallow and carefully dip it all the way into the melted candy until the marshmallow is completely covered. Gently tap off the excess candy, place the dipped marshmallow on the lined baking tray and decorate it with the sprinkles.

Repeat until all of the marshmallows have been dipped and decorated, then set them aside to dry. Once they are all dry, transfer them to mini cupcake cases. Store in a tin or an airtight container for up to a week.

CHOCOLATE & CHESTNUT MERINGUES

These meringue kisses are inspired by the classic 'Mont Blanc' combination of chocolate, chestnut and cream. Once assembled, they can be quite tricky to transport, so why not take them with you to a friend's house in their separate components, and have fun serving them up as a DIY dessert.

MAKES 25

FOR THE MERINGUES
2 large (US – extra large) egg
    whites
100 g (3½ oz/⅖ cup)
    caster (superfine) sugar

FOR THE GANACHE
60 ml (2 fl oz) double (thick) cream
60 g (2 oz) dark chocolate

FOR THE CHESTNUT CREAM
125 ml (4 fl oz) double (thick)
    cream
3 tablespoons chestnut spread

Preheat the oven to 140°C (275°F/gas mark 1) and line 2 baking trays with baking paper.

Whisk the egg whites in a food processor (make sure that the bowl is completely grease free) until they're foamy. Gradually add the sugar to the foamy egg whites, and continue whisking until the mixture forms stiff, glossy peaks. Transfer the mixture to a piping bag fitted with a 1 cm (½ in) round nozzle. Holding the bag vertically so that the tip is 1 cm (½ in) above the tray, pipe approximately 50 small rounds until all of the mixture is used up.

Turn the oven down to 120°C (248°F/ less than gas mark 1). Bake for 45 minutes, or until the shells of the meringues are crisp. Turn the oven off and leave the cooked meringues in the oven, with the door shut, until it has fully cooled and the meringues have dried out.

To make the ganache, heat the cream in a saucepan over a medium heat until it is bubbling. In a clean bowl, break up the chocolate and pour the cream over the top of it. Whisk the chocolate and cream until the mixture is smooth and all of the chocolate is melted. Set the chocolate mixture aside to cool, and then chill for 20 minutes, or until the mixture has thickened.

Once the mixture has thickened, beat it with a spatula until smooth.

To make the chestnut cream, use a food processor to whisk the cream until it forms soft peaks. Fold in the chestnut spread until it is just incorporated, showing a ripple of chestnut through the mixture.

To assemble these trEATs, spoon a small amount of the ganache onto the bottom of one meringue and a small amount of the chestnut cream onto the bottom of another, and then sandwich them together. Chill them in the fridge for up to a day or eat straight away. Store the meringues (without the ganache or chestnut cream) in a tin or an airtight container for up to 3 days.

CINNAMON HOT CHOCOLATE SPOONS

These hot chocolate spoons make a cosy gift for hot chocolate fans. To serve, place the spoon in a cup, pour over 120 ml (4 fl oz) of steaming hot milk, and stir. The marshmallows melt into the drink and bring just enough sweetness to the cinnamon-spiced dark chocolate.

MAKES 12

200 g (7 oz) dark chocolate,
  finely chopped
2 teaspoons ground cinnamon,
  plus extra for sprinkling
36 mini marshmallows
12 wooden teaspoons

Heat the chocolate in a glass bowl over a saucepan of simmering water, ensuring that the water doesn't touch the bottom of the bowl. Stir until the chocolate is almost melted, then remove the pan from the heat. Remove the glass bowl from the saucepan to ensure that the chocolate doesn't become overheated, and continue to stir the chocolate until it is completely melted.

Allow the chocolate to cool slightly before stirring in the cinnamon.

Then, pour the chocolate mixture into a 12-hole silicone ice-cube tray, filling each hole three-quarters full. Leave the chocolate to set for 5 minutes, then carefully press 3 mini marshmallows and a wooden spoon into each cube.

Dust with the remaining cinnamon and chill in the fridge for 2 hours, or until completely firm.

Turn the chocolate out of the ice-cube tray, and wrap in cellophane bags, or store in a tin or an airtight container for up to 2 weeks.

BACON & PECAN NUT CHOCOLATE SHARDS

The saltiness of the bacon works brilliantly with the sweetness of the chocolate in this recipe, making these shards a deliciously daring trEAT for your adventurous friends. Stack up the shard shapes in cellophane bags tied with dark pink or red stripy ribbon, and watch the surprise on your friends' faces as they bite into these savoury sweets.

MAKES 15 SHARDS

6 rashers smoked streaky bacon
50 g (2 oz) pecan nuts, roughly
   chopped
200 g (7 oz) dark chocolate,
   finely chopped

Preheat the grill to a medium setting.

Line a baking tray with foil. Place the bacon on the tray and grill for 10 minutes, or until crisp. Transfer the bacon onto some kitchen paper on a plate, and set it aside to cool and dry. Then, roughly chop the bacon.

Meanwhile, line a baking tray with baking paper. Heat the chocolate in a glass bowl over a saucepan of simmering water, ensuring that the water does not touch the bottom of the bowl. Stir the chocolate until it is almost melted, then remove the pan from the heat. Remove the glass bowl from the saucepan to ensure that the chocolate doesn't become overheated, and continue to stir until the chocolate is completely melted. Allow the chocolate to cool slightly before pouring it onto the lined tray.

Spread the chocolate evenly over the baking tray using a palate knife, and sprinkle the bacon and pecans on top. Chill the mixture in the fridge until the chocolate has set, then cut it into about 15 shards using a sharp knife.

Wrap the shards in cellophane to keep them fresh, or a tin or airtight container. Store in the fridge and eat or within 2 days.

WHITE CHOCOLATE & PISTACHIO POPCORN

I first made this popcorn for a New Year's Eve party, and I can report that it was polished off well before midnight! The combination is salty, sweet and unexpected for popcorn. Package it up in pistachio-green paper cones and pretty bags, or show it off in a big jar.

MAKES 300 G (10½ OZ)

2 tablespoons vegetable oil
60 g (2 oz) popcorn kernels
200 g (7 oz) white chocolate, finely chopped
50 g (2 oz) pistachio nuts, roughly chopped
½ teaspoon sea salt

Line 2 baking trays with baking paper.

Heat the oil in a large saucepan with a lid over a medium heat. Add the popcorn kernels and continue to heat, shaking the pan occasionally to ensure nothing sticks, for 5 minutes, or until all of the popcorn has popped. Transfer it to the prepared trays.

Next, heat the chocolate in a glass bowl over a saucepan of simmering water, ensuring that the water doesn't touch the bottom of the bowl. Stir until the chocolate is almost melted, then remove the pan from the heat. Remove the glass bowl from the saucepan to ensure that the chocolate doesn't become overheated, and continue to stir the chocolate until it has completely melted. Allow the chocolate to cool slightly before drizzling it over the popcorn. Then, sprinkle the pistachios and salt over the top.

Chill your popcorn creation in the fridge until the chocolate has fully set, then break up any bits of stuck-together popcorn and portion it into bags, or store in an airtight jar or tin. You can store it for up to 3 days, but it is best eaten fresh.

CHOCOLATE ROSE TRUFFLES

These romantic and subtly flavoured truffles make a chic gift paired with a simple bunch of roses. The recipe follows the same method as for the Salted Caramel Truffles (page 102), but swaps out the salted caramel for the rose-flavoured cream.

MAKES 40

200 ml (7 fl oz) double (thick) cream
3 drops rose extract
200 g (7 oz) dark chocolate, finely chopped
50 g (2 oz) cocoa powder

Heat the cream in a saucepan over a medium heat until small bubbles appear, then add the rose extract.

Place the chopped chocolate in a bowl and pour the cream over it. Gently whisk the mixture until it is completely smooth and all of the chocolate has melted. Set your chocolate mixture aside to cool, then chill for at least 1 hour, or until it is firm enough to roll into balls.

Place the cocoa powder in a shallow bowl. Coat your fingers in the cocoa, then scoop out around 10 g (½ oz) of the truffle mixture at a time and roll it into balls. Roll each ball in the cocoa to coat it, then place it in an airtight container, cellophane bags or a tin to store. Chill the truffles in the fridge until you're ready to give or eat them (they keep for up to a week).

SALTED CARAMEL
TRUFFLES

This recipe uses the deliciously dark and buttery Salted Caramel Sauce from page 89. The result is a satisfyingly squidgy truffle, which is dipped in chocolate to maintain its shape.

MAKES 40

FOR THE TRUFFLES
240 ml (8½ fl oz) Salted
   Caramel Sauce (page 89)
200 g (7 oz) dark chocolate,
   finely chopped
50 g (2 oz) cocoa powder

FOR THE CHOCOLATE
COATING
160 g (5⅖ oz) dark chocolate,
   finely chopped
sea salt or gold lustre dust to
   decorate

Heat the salted caramel in a small saucepan over a medium heat until it is bubbling. Place the chopped chocolate in a clean bowl and pour the caramel over the chocolate, gently whisking until the mixture is smooth and all of the chocolate has melted. Set the chocolate mixture aside to cool and chill for at least 1 hour, or until it's firm enough to roll it into balls.

Once your chocolate mixture is firm, place the cocoa in a shallow bowl. Coat your fingers in the cocoa, and then scoop out around 10 g (½ oz) of the truffle mixture at a time and roll it into balls. Roll each ball in the cocoa until it is coated. Once you have coated all of the truffles, chill them in the fridge for 15 minutes.

To prepare your chocolate coating, first line a baking tray with baking paper. Heat the chocolate in a glass bowl over a pan of simmering water, ensuring that the water doesn't touch the bottom of the bowl. Stir until the chocolate is almost melted, then remove the pan from the heat. Remove the glass bowl from the saucepan to ensure that the chocolate doesn't become overheated, and continue to stir until the chocolate is completely melted.

Allow the chocolate to cool a little, then, using a toothpick, dip the truffles into it one at a time. Shake off the excess chocolate, set the truffles on the tray and decorate with the sea salt or gold lustre dust before they dry. Store your truffles in an airtight container in the fridge until you're ready to give or eat them.

APPLE & CINNAMON COMPOTE

The cinnamon in this compote gives it a delicious apple-pie flavour. Serve the compote with yoghurt or ice cream, like the Rhubarb & Vanilla version on page 104, or try it chilled and spread onto buttered bread.

FILLS 2 × 250 ML (8½ FL OZ) JARS

700 g (1 lb 8½ oz/about 8 apples) Granny Smith apples, peeled, cored and chopped into 1-cm (½-in) cubes
1 teaspoon ground cinnamon
8 tablespoons water
8 tablespoons caster (superfine) sugar

Heat the apples, cinnamon, water and half of the sugar in a saucepan with a lid. Bring to the boil and then simmer over a low heat, shaking the pan occasionally to make sure that the fruit doesn't stick to the bottom. Cook the mixture for 20 minutes, or until the apples are soft. Taste the compote and add the remaining sugar if it is needed. Set aside to cool.

Using a food processor, blend the mixture to a smooth texture, then divide between two clean jars. Seal and store in the fridge and eat within a week.

RHUBARB & VANILLA COMPOTE

Rhubarb is one of my all-time favourite ingredients. This compote is so easy to make, and has a beautiful translucent pink colour. Keep a jar for yourself and eat it with yoghurt, granola or ice cream, and make the other one into a pretty gift by tying a spoon to the side.

Fills 2 × 250 ml (8½ fl oz) jars

500 g (1 lb 2 oz) rhubarb, trimmed and chopped into 5-cm (2-in) chunks
250 g (9 oz/2 cups) caster (superfine) sugar
½ vanilla pod, split in half lengthways and seeds scraped out

Place the rhubarb, sugar and vanilla seeds in a saucepan with a lid. Stir the mixture to combine the ingredients, and then set aside for 20 minutes to release the juices.

Heat the mixture in the saucepan over a high heat. Bring to the boil and then simmer over a low heat, shaking the pan occasionally, for about 10–15 minutes, or until the rhubarb is tender but still keeps its shape. Allow the mixture to fully cool, then divide between two clean jars. Seal and store in the fridge, and eat within a week.

LEMON & BLACKBERRY JELLY

These lemony jellies make a fun after-dinner dessert gift. They can be transported in their moulds, or made in jam jars for sharing, topped with extra berries and lids.

5 leaves (9 g/½ oz) gelatine,
   cut into small pieces
100 ml (3½ fl oz) cold water
juice and grated zest of 2 lemons
50 g (2 oz) blackberries, halved,
   plus extra for serving
150 g (5 oz/⅔ cup) caster
   (superfine) sugar

Place the gelatine in a small bowl with the cold water, and set aside to soak for 10 minutes.

Meanwhile, heat the lemon juice and zest, blackberries and sugar in a small saucepan over a medium heat and bring to a simmer, stirring until the sugar has dissolved. Remove the pan from the heat and add the softened gelatine and water, stirring until the gelatine has melted. Pour the mixture through a sieve into a measuring jug and top up with water to make 500 ml (17 fl oz) of liquid.

Divide the mixture between 6 x 100 ml (3½ fl oz) moulds, or 3 jam jars. Add 3 or 4 blackberry halves and chill for 2 hours, or until the jelly has set.

To create a two-layer effect, make one third of the jelly as above and allow it to set. Make the remaining jelly in the same way but without the blackberries. Top up the moulds or jam jars with the lemon liquid and chill again to finish.

Cover and store in the fridge for up to 3 days.

POMEGRANATE &
VANILLA VODKA

This recipe makes enough flavoured vodka for two small bottles. Find attractive, swing-top bottles online, and personalise them with a favourite cocktail suggestion on a hand-written label.

Makes 500 ml (17 fl oz)

75 g (2½ oz/⅓ cup) caster (superfine) sugar
½ vanilla pod
5 tablespoons water
1 pomegranate, seeds removed
500 ml (17 fl oz) vodka

Heat the sugar, vanilla and water in a saucepan. Bring to the boil and simmer for 4–5 minutes, or until the sugar has dissolved. Set the mixture aside to cool.

Meanwhile, remove the seeds from the pomegranate: cut the fruit in half, hold over a bowl and give it a satisfying bash with the back of a wooden spoon. Then, place the cooled syrup, vanilla pod, pomegranate and vodka in a large, clean sterilised jar with a lid, and shake to combine the ingredients. Place the jar somewhere cool and dark for a week, shaking occasionally to let the flavours infuse.

When the week is up, pour the flavoured vodka through a sieve. Divide the vodka between two clean 250 ml (8½ fl oz) bottles. Add some fresh pomegranate seeds to each bottle and seal. Store somewhere cool and dark for up to a month.

MINI GINGERBREAD HOUSES
TEMPLATE

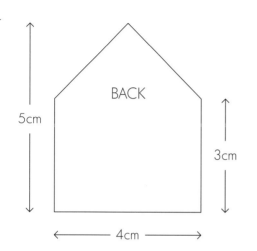

BACK

5cm

3cm

4cm

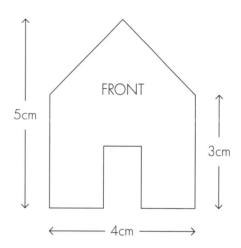

FRONT

5cm

3cm

4cm

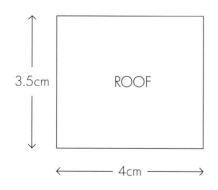

ROOF

3.5cm

4cm

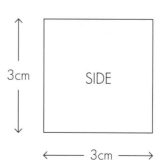

SIDE

3cm

3cm

INDEX

STOCKISTS

Ribbon, craft paper, parcel tags, rubber stamp sets and tissue paper:

UK	AUSTRALIA	US
www.liberty.co.uk	www.kikki-k.com	www.hobbylobby.com
www.notonthehighstreet.com	www.shop.cottonon.com/shop/typo	www.michaels.com
www.paperchase.co.uk	www.spotlight.com.au	www.paper-source.com

Baker's twine, paper bags, egg cartons and wooden spoons:

UK	AUSTRALIA	US
www.peachblossom.co.uk	www.shop.paperpoint.com.au	www.save-on-crafts.com
		www.shopsweetlulu.com

Unusual moulds and cake tins, jars and swing-top bottles:

UK	AUSTRALIA	US
www.divertimenti.co.uk	www.cakesaroundtown.com.au	www1.macys.com
www.lakeland.co.uk	www.kitchenwaredirect.com.au	www.specialtybottle.com

Cake boxes and deli bags:

UK	AUSTRALIA	US
cupcakeboxesuk.com	www.creativegiftpackaging.com	www.brpboxshop.com
www.carrierbagshop.co.uk		

Jars:

UK	AUSTRALIA	US
www.leparfait.co.uk	www.jamjarshop.com.au	www.specialtybottle.com
www.freemanharding.co.uk	www.glassbottles.biz	www.freshpreserving.com

Vintage tins and tea cups:

UK, Australia and US
www.ebay.co.uk
Local charity shops, car boot sales and flea markets

Cake decorating supplies, cake boxes and cellophane bags:

UK	AUSTRALIA	US
www.cakescookiesandcraftsshop.co.uk	bakingpleasures.com.au	cooksdream.com
www.loypack.com	www.cakedecoratingsolutions.com.au	sweetwise.com

Royal icing sugar, extracts and a good selection of home baking supplies:

UK	AUSTRALIA	US
www.waitrose.com	www.bakerysugarcraft.com.au	www.americanspice.com
		www.foodservicewarehouse.com
		www.kitchenkrafts.com

Violet extract and crystallised petals:

UK	AUSTRALIA	US
www.uncleroys.co.uk	bakingpleasures.com.au	www.herbspro.com
		www.marxfoods.com

ACKNOWLEDGEMENTS

It's been brilliant fun writing *trEATs* and I've been lucky to work with some great people. I'd especially like to thank Danielle Wood for the beautiful photographs, Kate Pollard, Kajal Mistry, Niki Foreman and the team at Hardie Grant, Anika Mistry for the design, my friends and family for their support, suggestions and enthusiastic recipe tasting, my mum for teaching me how to make scones all those years ago and my lovely husband, Alex.

APRIL CARTER

April Carter writes the baking blog *Rhubarb & Rose* and loves making beautiful and delicious treats for friends, family and special commissions. She lives in London and *trEATs* is her second book.
www.rhubarbandrose.co.uk

trEATs

First published 2013 by Hardie Grant Books

Hardie Grant Books (UK)
Dudley House, North Suite
34–35 Southampton Street
London WC2E 7HF
www.hardiegrant.co.uk

Hardie Grant Books (Australia)
Ground Floor, Building 1
658 Church Street
Melbourne, VIC 3121
www.hardiegrant.com.au

British Library Cataloguing-in-Publication Data. A catalogue record
for this book is available from the British Library.

ISBN 978-174270-6-344

Commissioning Editor: Kate Pollard
Desk Editor: Kajal Mistry
Photography © Danielle Wood
Blue floral image © iStockphoto LP 2010. All rights reserved.
Cover and Internal Design: Anika Mistry
Colour Reproduction by p2d

Printed and bound in China by 1010